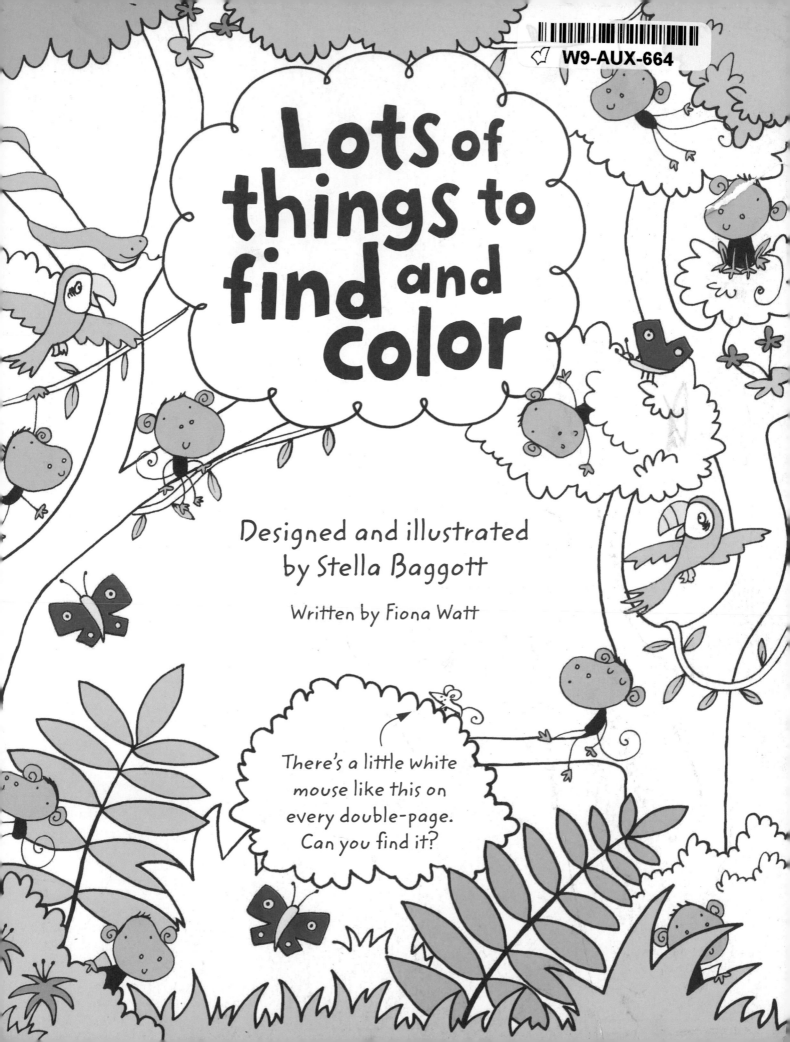

Lots of things to find and color

Designed and illustrated
by Stella Baggott

Written by Fiona Watt

There's a little white
mouse like this on
every double-page.
Can you find it?

Color all the
dinosaurs' teeth and
toenails yellow.

Find all the dragonflies
and color them with
bright colors.

Spot the odd one out in each row and color it in.

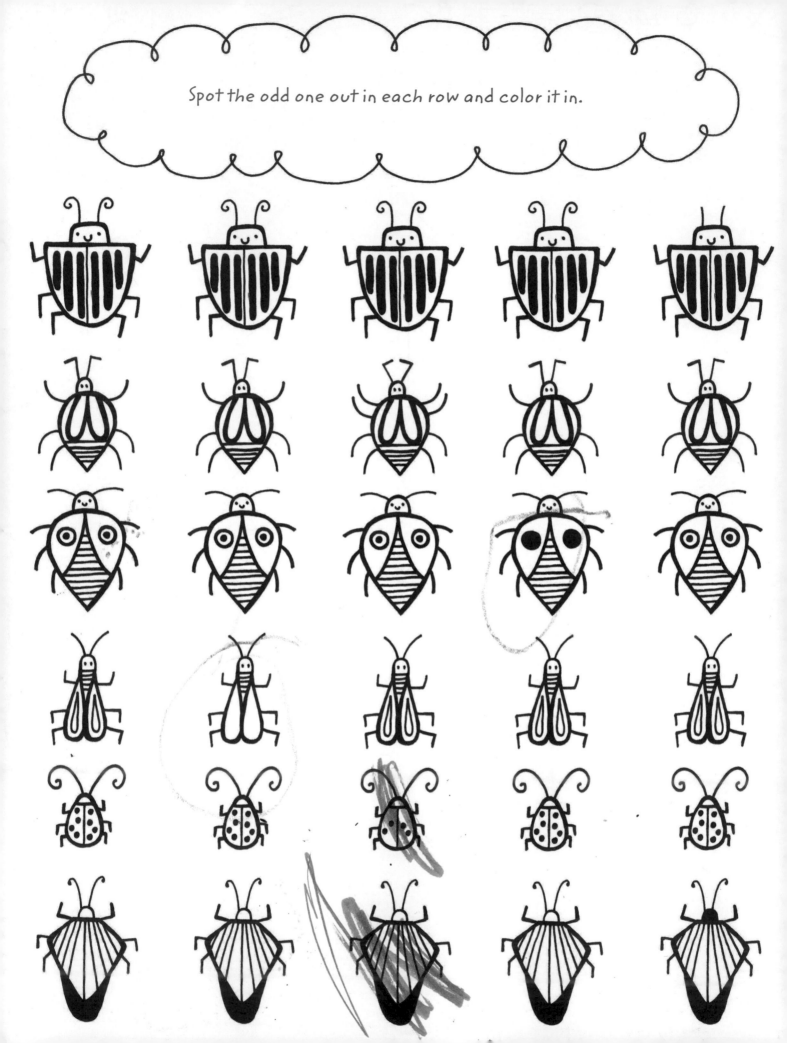

Draw stripes on all the cats that have whiskers.

Find the dogs hiding between the cats and color them.

Find all the striped fish and color them in.

Look for the submarines and color them blue.

Find the lighthouses and color the stripes red.

Find the cages with two birds inside and color in the birds.

Find the empty cage, then draw a bird inside it.

Copy the patterns onto the bottom elephant.

Can you find the bird hiding in the picture? Color it in.

Find each matching pair of birds and color them to match each other.

Which green path should Mr. Slug take through the apple to get to Mrs. Slug and their babies? Draw a line along it.

Find the finished face in each row and color it in.
Then, complete the other faces in the row.

Find the monkeys and color their faces, hands and feet.

Find the matching pictures and color them to match.

Find the chickens hidden in the picture and color their bodies yellow.

Color the chickens' beaks and head feathers red.

Can you find an egg?

Can you spot the car with suitcases on its roof?

Look for the signs with arrows and color them.

Find the lizards and color them green.

Color all the
cacti flowers in
bright colors.

Find five things that
aren't fish and
color them.

Draw patterns on
the plain fish.

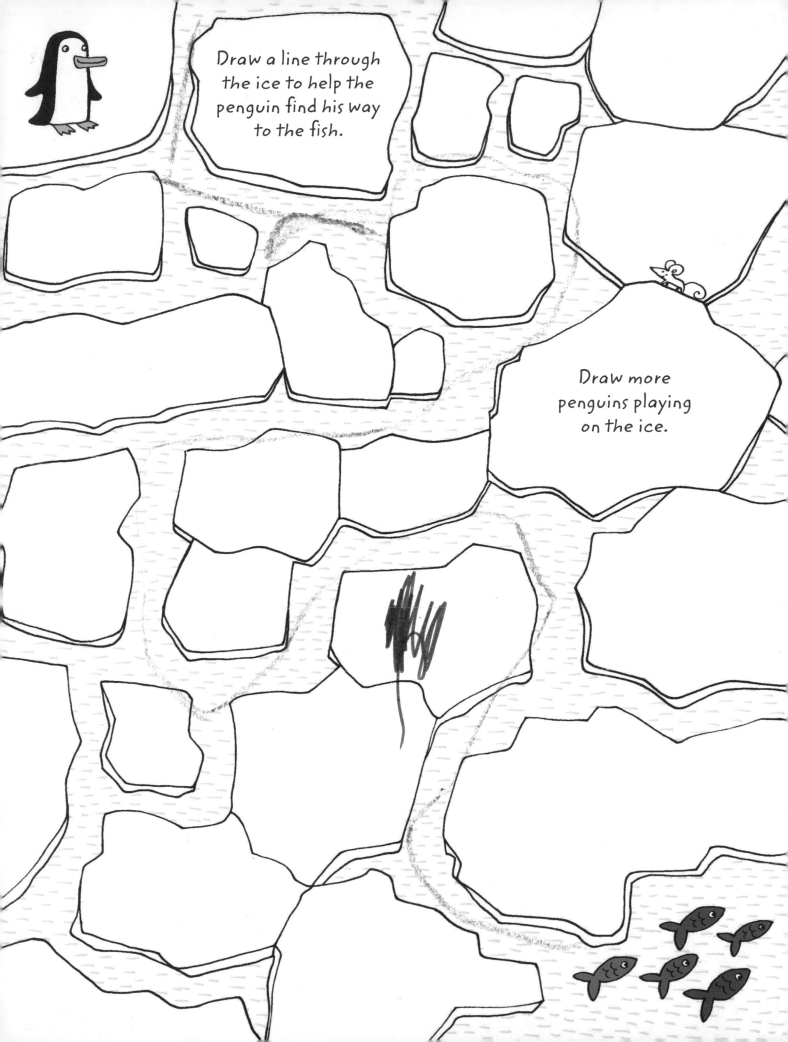

Draw a line through the ice to help the penguin find his way to the fish.

Draw more penguins playing on the ice.

Find all the aliens and color them green.

Color in all the astronauts who are on a spacewalk.

Draw more stars, planets and rockets to fill this page.

Color the rockets in bright colors.

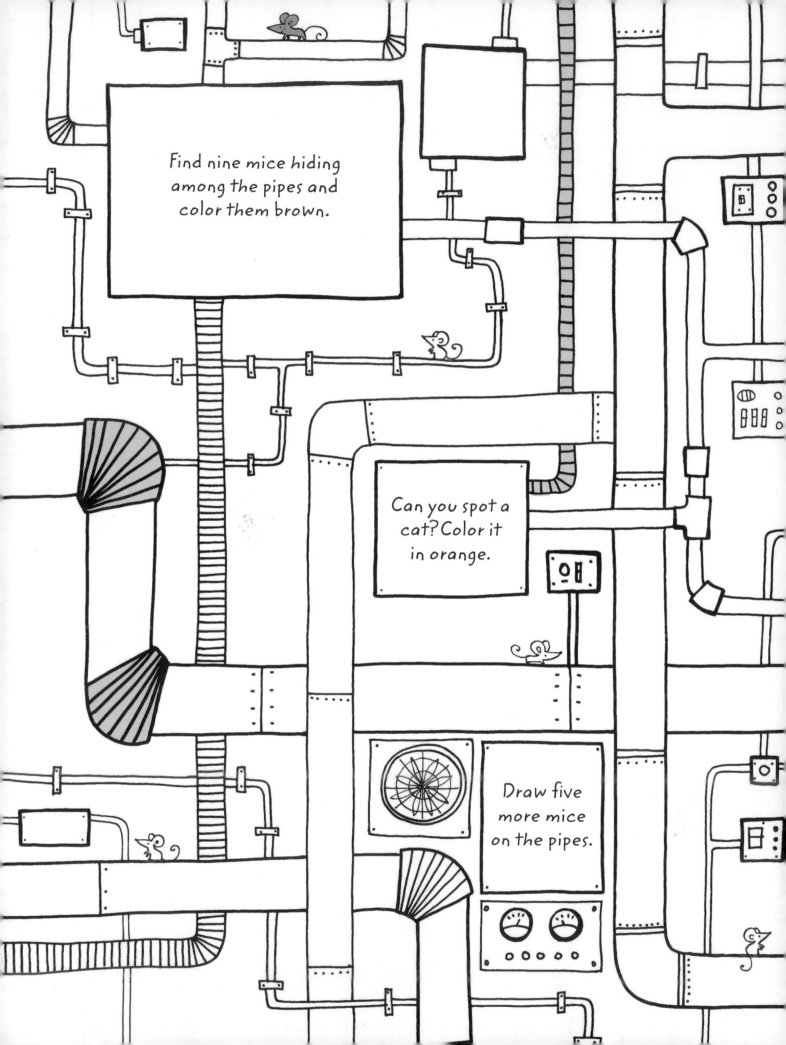

Find nine mice hiding among the pipes and color them brown.

Can you spot a cat? Color it in orange.

Draw five more mice on the pipes.

Copy the patterns onto the plain dolls and color them in.

Can you spot a bee painted on one of the dolls?

How many chameleons can you find hiding in the leaves?

Color the chameleons with bright stripes.

Can you spot a fly?

Find the birds with long tail feathers and color them.

Find all the ladybugs and color them red.

Can you spot a bee?

Find all the flowers that look like this, and color them pink.

Find the ladybugs with only two spots and color them red.

Find the ladybugs with four spots and color them orange.

Look for the ladybugs with six spots and color them yellow.

Find five more dogs hiding in
this picture and color them red
with yellow spots.

Find the finished cat or dog in each row and color it in.
Then, complete the other faces to match it.

Find the dolls with bows in their hair and color them red.

Spot the dolls with flowers in their hair and color them yellow.

Some of the dolls have patterned sashes. Color the dolls blue.

Find the fish and color them blue.

Fill in all the tadpoles that have grown two little legs.

Find the tadpole with arms and legs.

Find the dragonflies and color them.

Color in all the things that might belong to a pirate.

Find the crabs and color them red.

Spot all the seahorses and color them green.

Color all the starfish in the same color.

Find the mice wearing ballerina tutus and color them pink.

Find the mice wearing black top hats and color their bowties red.

Can you find and color a mouse reading a book?

Find the foxes hiding in the forest and color them orange.

Find all the birds and color them yellow.

Color in all the things that the chefs can use for cooking.

Find the fairies holding star wands and color their wings blue.

Look for the fairies holding flowers and color their dresses pink.

Spot the fairies wearing crowns and color their dresses yellow.

Color in all the snails.

Find all the
bones and color
them yellow.

Look for the dogs wearing collars, and color their collars.

Color in all the dogs that are running around.

Find the finished face in each row and color it in.
Then, finish the other faces.

Find the balls of
yarn and color
them purple.

Color in the cats
that are licking
their paws.

Find the
butterflies and
color them blue.

Find the flowers
like this, and
color them in.

Find the ladybugs and color them red.

Color all the bees yellow.

Copy these patterns onto the owls
sitting on the branch below.

Draw a line along the branches to show the way that the squirrel must go to reach the little acorn.

Can you spot the
mole eating a
strawberry? Color
the mole brown.

Find the moles wearing hats and color their hats.

Find the watering cans and color them red.

Find the robots with clocks on their tummies and color the clocks orange.

Look for all the robots with wheels and color them green.

Spot the robots with long, wavy arms. Color them red.

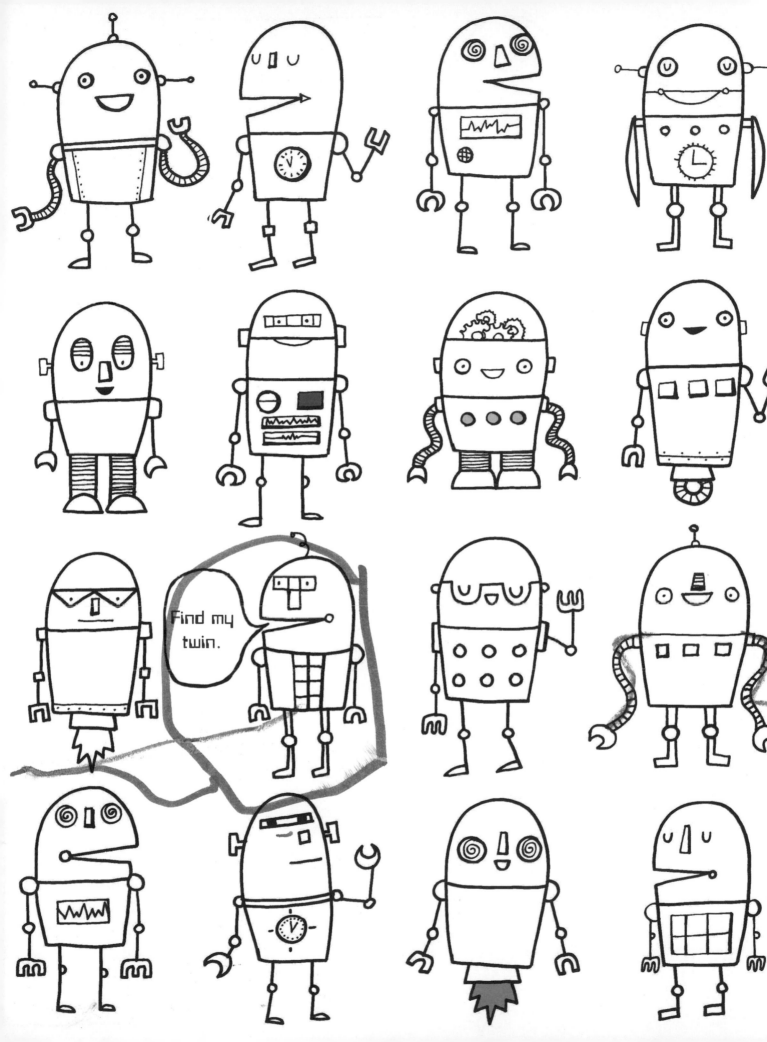

Find my twin.

Draw a line through the maze to show where the alien should fly to reach the green and purple planet.

Find five snakes wearing strange things and color in their bodies.

Look for the snakes with two fangs, then color the snakes.

Find the pairs of shoes and color them to match.

Add more bright spots
along the centipede's body.

Find all the treasure chests and color them.

Find the crab.

Spot the pirate hats with skulls and crossbones and color them gray.

Find the spotted headscarves and color them red.

Copy the patterns
onto the butterfly
below, then color
them in.

Find the vases with spiral patterns and color them.

Find the vases with three flowers and color the flowers yellow.

Look for the vases with four flowers and color the flowers orange.

Find three flowers like this, and color them.

Find the butterflies hiding among the flowers and color them in.

Can you find a fairy?

Find all the hats and fill them in with bright colors.

Can you find the squirrel who has fallen over?

Draw stripes on all the plain scarves.

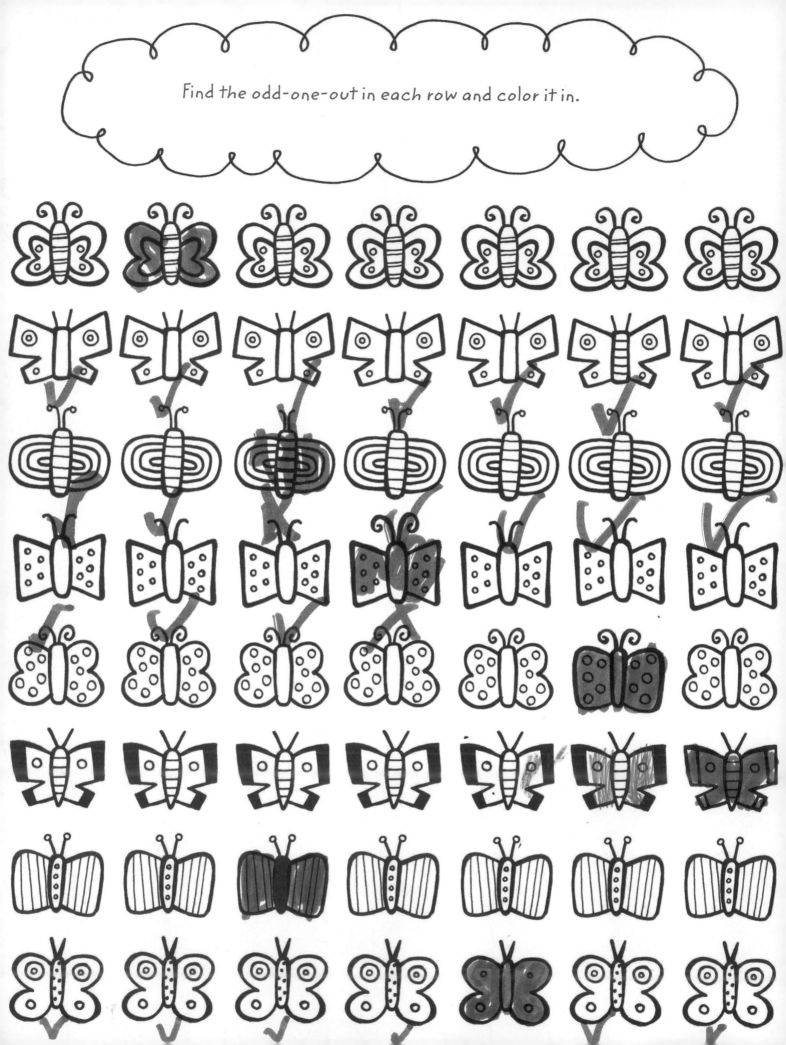

Find the odd-one-out in each row and color it in.

Find the
mermaids with
very curly ends
on their tails and
color them blue.

Draw a line to show the tunnels the rabbit can go down to get to her babies.

Draw some more worms in the soil.

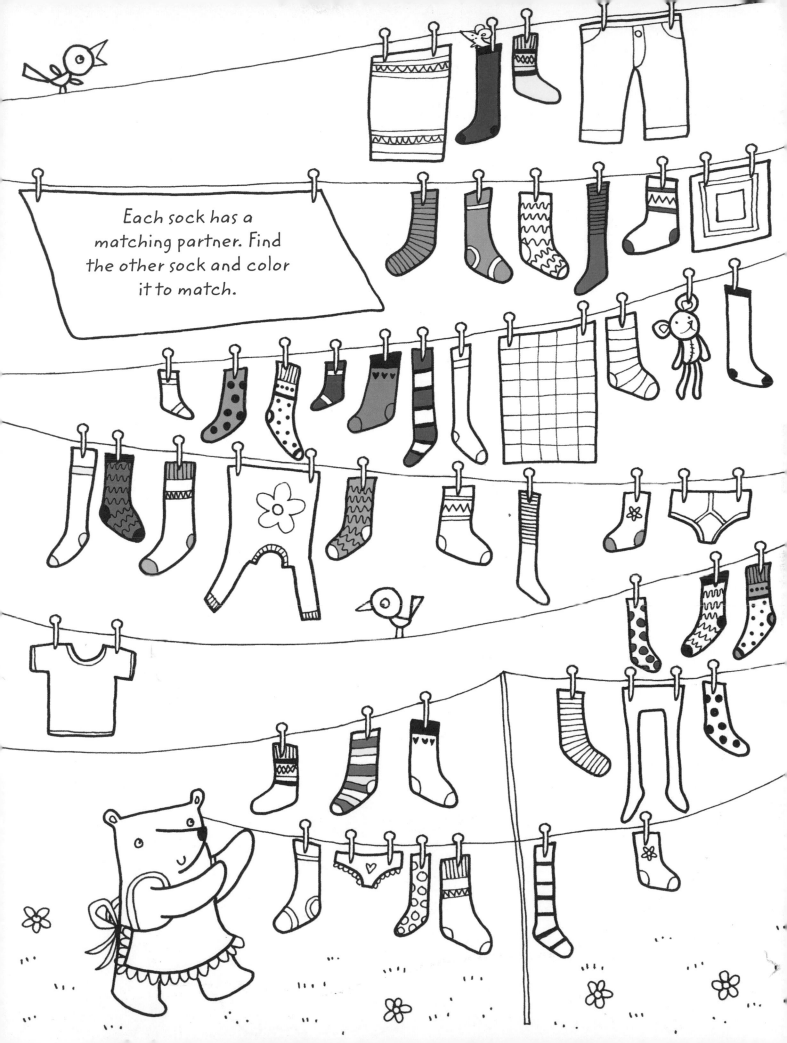

Each sock has a matching partner. Find the other sock and color it to match.

Find the planes with stars on their wings and color them in.

Can you spot the crocodile flying a plane? Color him green.

Spot a pilot wearing goggles.

Look for all the kites and color them in, too.

Draw lines to show the way Mr. Croc and Miss Kitty should go get to the mouse's house.

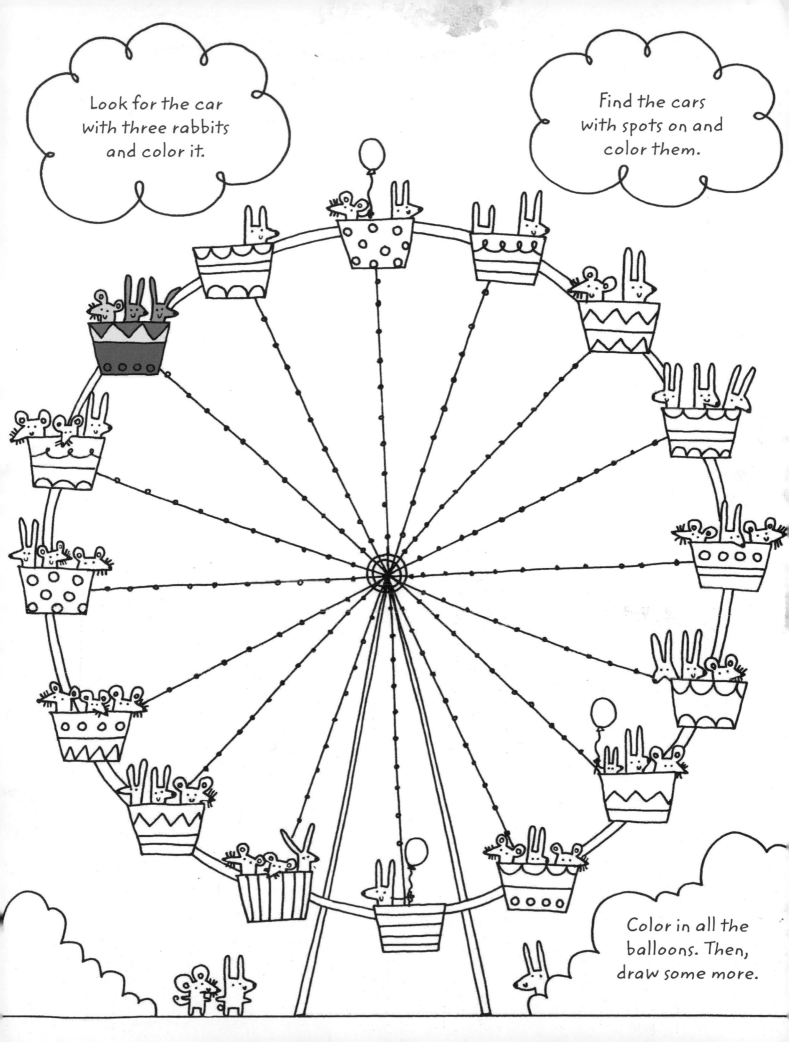

Look for the car with three rabbits and color it.

Find the cars with spots on and color them.

Color in all the balloons. Then, draw some more.

Find the pods with three peas inside and color the peas green.

Can you find the sleeping pea?